CW00402613

Fragments of Anaxagoras

by Anaxagoras, translated by John Burnet

TABLE OF CONTENTS

Fragments of Anaxagoras

Fragments according to the text and arrangement of Diels.

Fragment 1

All things were together, infinite both in number and in smallness; for the small too was infinite. And, when all things were together, none of them could be distinguished for their smallness. For air and aether prevailed over all things, being both of them infinite; for amongst all things these are the greatest both in quantity and size.[1]

Fragment 2

For air and aether are separated off from the mass that surrounds the world, and the surrounding mass is infinite in quantity.

Fragment 3

Nor is there a least of what is small, but there is always a smaller; for it cannot be that what is should cease to be by being cut.[2] But there is also always something greater than what is great, and it is equal to the small in amount, and, compared with itself, each thing is both great and small.

Fragment 4

And since these things are so, we must suppose that there are contained many things and of all sorts in the things that are uniting, seeds of all things, with all sorts of shapes and colours and savours, and that men have been formed in them, and the other animals that have life, and that these men have inhabited cities and cultivated fields as with us; and that they have a sun and a moon and the rest as with us; and that their earth brings forth for them many things of all kinds of which they gather the best together into their dwellings, and use them. Thus much have I said with regard to separating off, to show that it will not be only with us that things are separated off, but elsewhere too.

But before they were separated off, when all things were together, not even was any colour distinguishable; for the mixture of all things prevented it—of the moist and the dry; and the warm and the cold, and the light and the dark, and of much earth that was in it, and of a multitude of innumerable seeds in no way like each, other. For none of theother things either is like any Other. And these things being so, we must hold that all things are in the whole.[3]

Fragment 5

And those things having been thus decided, we must know that all of them are neither more nor less; for it is not possible for them to be more than all, and all are always equal.

Fragment 6

And since the portions of the great and of the small are equal in amount, for this reason, too, all things will be in everything; nor is it possible for them to be apart, but all things have a portion of everything. Since it is impossible for there to be a least thing, they cannot be separated, nor come to be by themselves; but they must be now, just as they were in the beginning, all-together. And in all things many things are contained, and an equal number both in the greater and in the smaller of the things that are separated off.

Fragment 7

. . . So that we cannot know the number of the things that are separated off, either in word or deed.

Fragment 8

The things that are in one world are not divided nor cut off from one another with a hatchet, neither the warm from the cold nor the cold from the warm.

Fragment 9

. . . as these things revolve and are separated off by the force and swiftness. And the swiftness makes the force. Their swiftness is not like the swiftness of any of the things that are now among men, but in every way many times as swift.

Fragment 10

How can hair come from what is not hair, or flesh from what is not flesh?

Fragment 11

In everything there is a portion of everything except Nous, and there are some things in which there is Nous also.

Fragment 12

All other things partake in a portion of everything, while Nous is infinite and self-ruled, and is mixed with nothing, but is alone itself by itself. For if it were not by itself, but were mixed with anything else, it would partake in all things if it were mixed with any; for in everything there is a portion of everything, as has been said by me in what goes before, and the things mixed with it would hinder it, so that it would have power over nothing in the same way that it has now being alone by itself. For it is the thinnest of all things and the purest, and it has all knowledge about everything and the greatest strength; and Nous has power over all things, both greater and smaller, that have life. And Nous had power over the whole revolution, so that it began to revolve in the beginning. And it began to revolve first from a small beginning; but the revolution now extends over a larger space, and will extend over a larger still. And all the things that are mingled together and separated off and distinguished are all known by Nous. And Nous set in order all things that were to be, and all things that were and are not now and that are, and this revolution in which now revolve the stars and the sun and the moon, and the air and the aether that are separated off. And this revolution caused the separating off, and the rare is separated off from the dense, the warm from the cold, the light from the dark, and the dry from the moist. And there are many portions in many things. But no thing is altogether separated off nor distinguished from anything else except Nous. And all Nous is alike, both the greater and the smaller; while nothing else is like anything else, but each single thing is and was most manifestly those things of which it has most in it.

Fragment 13

And when Nous began to move things, separating off took place from all that was moved, and so much as Nous set in motion was separated. And as things were set in motion and separated, the revolution caused them to be separated much more.

Fragment 14

And Nous, which ever is, is certainly there, where everything else is, in the surrounding mass, and in what has been united with it and separated off from it.[4]

Fragment 15

The dense and the moist and the cold and the dark came together where the earth is now, while the rare and the warm and the dry (and the bright) went out towards the further part of the aether.[5]

Fragment 16

From these as they are separated off earth is solidified; for from mists water is separated off, and from water earth. From the earth stones are solidified by the cold, and these rush outwards more than water.

Fragment 17

The Hellenes follow a wrong usage in speaking of coming into being and passing away; for nothing comes into being or passes away, but there is mingling and separation of things that are. So they would be right to call coming into being mixture, and passing away separation.

Fragment 18

It is the sun that puts brightness into the moon.

Fragment 19

We call rainbow the reflexion of the sun in the clouds. (Now it is a sign of storm; for the water that flows round the cloud causes wind or pours down in rain.)

Fragment 20

With the rise of the Dogstar (?) men begin the harvest; with its setting they begin to till the fields. It is hidden for forty days and nights.

Fragment 21

From the weakness of our senses we are not able to judge
the truth.

Fragment 21a

What appears is a vision of the unseen.

Fragment 21b

(We can make use of the lower animals) because we use our own experience and memory and wisdom and art.

Fragment 22

What is called "birds' milk" is the white of the egg.

Notes

1 ↑ Simplicius tells us this was at the beginning of Book I. The sentence quoted by Diog. ii. 6 (R. P. 153) is not a fragment of Anaxagoras, but a summary, like the πάντα ῥεῖ ascribed to Herakleitos." (Chap. III. p. 146).

2 ↑ Zeller's τομῇ still seems to me a convincing correction of the MS. τὸ μή, which Diels retains.

3 ↑ I had already pointed out in the first edition that Simplicius quotes this three times as a continuous fragment, and that we are not entitled to break it up. Diels now prints it as a single passage.

4 ↑ Simplicius gives fr. 14 thus (p. 157, 5); ὁ δὲ νοῦς ὅσα ἐστί τε κάρτα καὶ νῦν ἐστιν. Diels now reads ὁ δὲ νοῦς ὃς ἀ<εἰ> ἐστί τὸ κάρτα καὶ νῦν ἐστιν. The correspondence of ἀεὶ . . . καὶ νῦν is strongly in favour of this.

5 ↑ On the text of fr. 15, see R. P. 156 a. I have followed Schorn in adding καὶ τὸ λαμπρόν from Hippolytos.

Note from the Editor

Odin's Library Classics strives to bring you unedited and unabridged works of classical literature. As such, this is the complete and unabridged version of the original English text unless noted. In some instances, obvious typographical errors have been corrected. This is done to preserve the original text as much as possible. The English language has evolved since the writing and some of the words appear in their original form, or at least the most commonly used form at the time. This is done to protect the original intent of the author. If at any time you are unsure of the meaning of a word, please do your research on the etymology of that word. It is important to preserve the history of the English language.

Taylor Anderson

Printed in Great Britain
by Amazon

62190138R00020